SAN FRANCISCO

Soaring a mile through the air over the narrow entrance to San Francisco Bay, the Golden Gate Bridge symbolizes the vigor of a venturesome city. The Ferry Building, on the previous page, has welcomed visitors to San Francisco since 1898.

THIS BEAUTIFUL WORLD   VOL. 17

SAN FRANCISCO

by PAUL C. JOHNSON

photographs by
Thomas Tracy,
Baron Wolman,
and others

講談社

Published by
KODANSHA INTERNATIONAL LTD.
Tokyo, Japan & Palo Alto, Calif., U.S.A.

PHOTO CREDITS

American Conservatory Theater, 101, 102; California Historical Society, 9; Robert Cameron, 19; Frances Coleberd, 21, 106; Carolyn Mason Jones, 105; George Knight, 49; Francis Mair, 16, 40, 52, 120; Betty Randall, half-title page, 31; Redwood Empire Association, 1, 45, 79; San Francisco Ballet Company, 103, 104; San Francisco Convention and Visitors Bureau, 6, 17, 29, 30, 38, 39, 44, 48, 66, 67, 97, 98, 107, 110; San Francisco Museum of Art, 96; San Francisco Port Commission, 22, 25, 26; Jacques Segal, 55; Thomas Tracy, front cover, frontispiece, 3, 4, 5, 11, 15, 18, 20, 27, 32, 33, 34, 35, 36, 37, 46, 47, 50, 51, 54, 56, 57, 58, 59, 60, 61, 62, 63, 64, 68, 69, 70, 71, 74, 75, 76, 80, 81, 82, 85, 86, 87, 88, 89, 90, 91, 92, 93, 95, 99, 100, 108, 112, 113, 114, 115, 117, 118, 119, 121, 122, back cover; United States Navy, 24; Vano-Wells-Fagliano, 10; Wells-Fargo Bank History Room, 7, 72; Baron Wolman, 2, 12, 13, 14, 23, 28, 41, 42, 43, 53, 73, 77, 78, 83, 84, 94, 109, 111, 116; Nathan Zabarsky, 65. Graphics coordination and layout: Judith Whipple.

Distributed in the British Commonwealth (excluding Canada and the Far East) by Ward Lock & Company Ltd., London and Sydney; in Continental Europe by Boxerbooks, Inc., Zurich; and in the Far East by Japan Publications Trading Co., C.P.O. Box 722, Tokyo. Published by Kodansha International Ltd., 2-12-21, Otowa, Bunkyo-ku, Tokyo, Japan and Kodansha International/USA, Ltd., 577 College Avenue, Palo Alto, California 94306. Copyright in Japan 1970, by Kodansha International Ltd. All rights reserved. Printed in Japan.

  Library of Congress Catalog Card No. 78-117381
  SBN 87011-120-5
  JBC No. 0326-781525-2361
First edition, 1970

CONTENTS

1. *The core* of San Francisco rises in tiers from the Civic Center to Nob and Russian Hills, crowned by a cathedral and myriads of high-rise apartments.

SAN FRANCISCO

THE BONNY MERRY CITY

No city in California—indeed, few in the world—can match the grandeur and exhilaration of San Francisco's natural setting.

Perched on the tip of a hilly peninsula, guarding the entrance to one of the great natural harbors of the world, its face to the setting sun and the Orient, San Francisco is called by destiny to be a great port city.

It is a compact metropolis, compressed into a small square, seven miles to a side. The wind-washed buildings, tightly packed into the 49-square-mile area, are spread over forty-two hills. Over this rumpled landscape, the city's first surveyor imposed the checkerboard street plan for a level town, thereby creating for all time the heart-stopping ups and downs that give a rollercoaster thrill to travel on the vertical thoroughfares.

The hills contribute a subtle psychological boost to the energies of the city. To every hill dweller, each day's climb is an achievement, each panting stop for breath an opportunity to soak up a view, and each summit a minor conquest. In a small, cumulative way, every hill resident is tested and stretched a little every day as he copes with his precipitous environment.

If the hills are a part of the collective psyche, so too is the stimulating climate, unpredictable and capricious, often compressing a year's seasons into a single day. There are some constants, however: the weather is generally cool in summer and foggy by spells throughout the year because of the city's location at the entrance to a great air trough between the ocean and the warm inland valleys. When

7

SAN FRANCISCO 🌿

the interior is hot, the heated air sucks cool ocean winds through the Golden Gate. The cooler air condenses into the familiar mists that are a tonic feature of the city's weather. The fog usually forms in the afternoon and its long finger can be seen probing across the bay to the opposite shore. The fog rolls in at two hundred feet or so, obscuring the deck of the Golden Gate Bridge, bathing the hills in mist and occasionally sinking to water level.

Challenged daily by their hills, sped on their way by the exhilarating chill, San Franciscans expend more than their share of energy and enterprise. A city built on maritime commerce—one third of its perimeter is wharfage—much of its energies are funneled into trade with the nations of the Pacific Basin and the complex financing of international commerce. Enhancing the cosmopolitan traditions of a port city that has been trafficking with the peoples of the world for more than a century, a score of national and ethnic enclaves contribute a rich cultural diversity to the city's charisma. Of such communities, Chinatown, Little Italy, and Japantown are the most familiar to the tourist, but no less influential are the dispersed colonies of French, German, Irish, Basque, Portuguese, and Mexican descendants of the founders of the modern city. The unusually large number of individuals with close ties to foreign lands flavors the city's cuisine, pageantry, and commerce, and encourages an off-hand tolerance for deviations in customs and beliefs. It is no accident that the United Nations was born here.

San Franciscans cherish the city's raffish past and blend it comfortably with the present. Many older buildings have been spared from the wrecking crane and nostalgically converted into modern offices, stores, and restaurants, and whole neighborhoods of Victorian gingerbread have been spruced up with paint and polish.

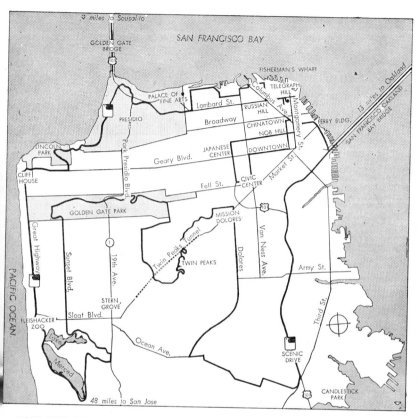

TIPS FOR TOURISTS

Bring warm clothing, any month of the year—especially summer.

Bring good walking shoes.

Plan your first cable car ride for mid-morning or mid-afternoon in midweek, to avoid crowds.

For advance information, write to the San Francisco Convention & Visitors Bureau, Fox Plaza, San Francisco, California 94102.

For a sample of the city, ride all three cable cars to the end of the line and back.

For a more thorough introduction, call Gray Line (see yellow pages).

For a self-guided tour, ask the Convention & Visitors Bureau for the map of their 49-Mile Drive. It is actually 70 miles long and is a full day's driving.

For a tour of the bay, call Harbor Tours (see yellow pages).

9

SAN FRANCISCO ⚜

The banker rides to his stainless steel skyscraper in an 1883 cable car. Millionaires dine out in a transformed utility substation. A 1924 ferry boat, a 1905 flatiron building, and an 1863 theater are changed respectively into offices for an industrial design firm, an advertising agency, and a flamboyant lawyer.

Along with a reverential appreciation of the past, the San Franciscan never permits nostalgia to impede an energetic attack on the present or an attempt to bend the future to his ends. Whole sections of the city are flattened to make way for mind-boggling residential and business complexes. The imagination and daring that thirty years ago created the great bridges in the face of corrosive skepticism is today driving to completion a vast rapid transit system that will, hopefully, ameliorate some of the region's traffic congestion.

The vitality of a restless people makes the city an exciting place to live and a fascinating spot to visit. Travelers are struck both by the spectacular setting and by the way it has been tamed. San Franciscans amuse themselves in cosmopolitan ways and they enjoy sharing their pleasures with newcomers. Matchless restaurants, stores, theaters, and galleries are always open to the visitor, all to be enjoyed in a setting where every street opens to a view of the storied hills, the ever-changing bay, or the perpetual light-show of alternating mist and sun.

3. *The setting:* Embraced by ocean and bay, the city partakes of both the pull of the tides of the world and the sheltered calm of the workaday port.

4. *The setting:* Fog pours ▶ through the Golden Gate, envelopes the city, endows the familiar with mystery, adds a snap to the air, and stirs to voice a melancholy chorus of foghorns.

13

5. *The setting:* Great spangled bridges leapfrog the bay, linking the city to other communities with bands of steel.

The Bay Bridge (1936) unites with the East Bay; the Golden Gate Bridge (1937), with the Redwood Empire.

17

6. *Spaniards* who founded San Francisco built
Mission Dolores (1782), a charming relic that has
survived fire, earthquake, and modernization.

BEGINNINGS OF AN ENTERPRISING CITY

Founded by Spanish colonizers in the same year as the Declaration of Independence in a move to block Russian settlers from occupying New Spain, San Francisco was destined from the start to play a major role in the history of the West Coast.

Surprisingly, discovery of the great bay itself came late. Spanish galleons had sailed past the Golden Gate since 1532 without once sighting the narrow entrance to the bay, and it remained for a land party to stumble on it in 1769 while searching for Monterey. Once revealed, the bay was immediately recognized as a strategic and commercial prize, and the Spaniards consolidated their find with a mission, a shoreside settlement, and a fort. For seventy-five years, they and their Mexican successors lived a pastoral life, supported by Indian labor, that was abruptly ended in 1846 when American naval forces raised the Stars and Stripes in the plaza, and tiny Yerba Buena became an American town, soon renamed San Francisco.

It dozed along until 1849, when the Gold Rush transformed it from a village of 439 souls into a brawling city of thirty-five thousand within a single year. So rapid was the city's growth that it outstripped the agencies of civil control, and for years the city was convulsed with alternating waves of lawlessness and reform. Despite this, the city acquired a monopolistic hold on the shipping, finance, and commerce of the emerging state of California.

On a fateful dawn in 1906, a cataclysmic earthquake and fire nearly destroyed the "bonny merry city." Undaunted, San Franciscans cleaned up the rubble, rebuilt the downed buildings; and "The City" resumed its rank as the leading metropolis of the West.

7. *Where a muddy shore-line* existed before, a town sprang into being to serve thousands of miners on their way to and from the gold fields. In this rendering from an 1852 daguerreotype, Montgomery Street is shown thronged with motley inhabitants drawn from all over the world. Montgomery Street was then the Embarcadero of its day, and store buildings backed up against the bay. Note the small boy fishing through a hole in the street.

8. *The never-sleeping eye* of the Vigilance Committee stared at evil-doers in Gold Rush San Francisco. Scoundrels, drawn by the easy pickings of gold-laden miners, infested the town until driven out by vigilantes in 1851, and again in 1856.

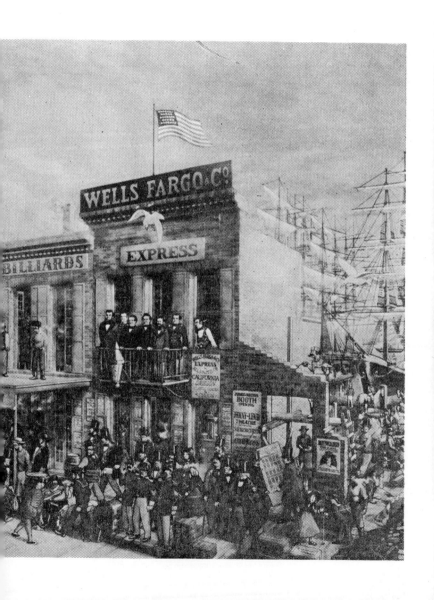

9. *A half-century's growth* following the Gold Rush went up in flames in 1906 when a titanic earthquake shook the city off its foundations and para-

lyzed fire fighting apparatus. The conflagration that followed raged for 72 hours, destroyed 512 blocks, $400 million of property, and 600 lives.

10. *Trademark* of the port, the clock tower of the Ferry Building, modeled on a Spanish prototype, was a teeming gateway for ferry-borne commuters from 1898 to 1936, and is now a trade center.

THE DYNAMIC WATERWORLD

The "port that built the city," as its promoters refer to it, is a dynamic scene with innumerable attractions for visitors.

Feverish activity ranges along the six miles of Embarcadero and on the water offshore. Every day sees an informal regatta take place on the bay, composed of vessels of all sizes and configurations, ranging from one-man skiffs to enormous aircraft carriers that barely squeak under the Golden Gate Bridge and announce their arrival with blasts on a powerful airhorn.

The waterfront officially starts on the north at the San Francisco Maritime Museum, a shiplike concrete structure, containing a remarkable collection of maritime exhibits, and swings past a floating museum of restored ships and the handsome square-rigged *Balclutha*, an eighty-year veteran of the Pacific trade.

Fisherman's Wharf, a tourist discovery since the 1920's, has been the home port of the fishing fleet since 1872. Now almost submerged in a sea of hot dog stands, souvenir shops, restaurants, and motels, the wharf still offers excellent seafood to those who know where to find it and an authentic contact with the workaday world of the fisherman.

Next in line to the south come the cargo and passenger piers. Cargoliners, flying the flags of every maritime nation, unload newsprint, copra, green coffee, and automobiles, and take aboard heavy machinery, agricultural products, and general merchandise. Passenger liners come and go with traditional fanfare, embarking on excursions that range from overnight sailings to Los Angeles to six-month round-the-world circuits. More than a hundred cruises

25

11. *Along the Embarcadero,* forty-two piers reach ▶
out into the bay from a seawall completed in the
1890's. Cargo, passenger, and naval vessels dock
at the finger piers, berthed with the help of
powerful tugs and unloaded by floating cranes.

depart each year, operated by two American-flag companies and four
flying the flags of Holland, Japan, Britain, and Taiwan.

Heart of the waterfront is the venerable Ferry Building, separating
odd- and even-numbered piers, and one-time entry point for
thousands of transbay commuters and passengers from transcon-
tinental trains. In service since 1898, the building lost its commuters
to the Bay Bridge in 1936 and is now a World Trade Center with
offices representing thirty foreign countries.

Connecting the long string of piers, the wide and chuckholed
Embarcadero carries an amazing conglomerate of vehicles. Mixed
with the usual torrent of automobiles are gargantuan cargo handlers,
huge truck-trailers laden with pipes, turbines, sacks of rice, crated
Bibles, and containerized goods, and the reluctant dragon of the
Belt Line Railroad that nudges its bulk through the streaming cars.

Originally, the waterfront was located some distance inland in
what is now the financial district, six blocks from the bay. When
the Forty-niners sailed into the harbor, they disembarked at the
corner of Clay and Montgomery Streets. Lacking adequate docking
facilities, ships' captains anchored their vessels in the mudflats, and
in time, a dead fleet of five hundred ships lay stranded there.

In the years that followed, tidal mud silted up the anchorages and
docks so rapidly that many wharves were almost useless. To correct
this, a seawall was started in 1878, formed largely of rock blasted
off the east face of Telegraph Hill. The wall moved the docks out
into deep water where they now are. In the process, 800 acres of
filled land were created for commercial development. As the port
grew, trade increased until by 1900 the harbor was the third busiest
in the world. It is still one of the leading ports on the coast, ranking
first in value of tonnage handled.

12—14. *In an atmosphere as savory* as chowder, live crabs are plopped into steam pots and cooked to the color of terra-cotta, the signal that their delicate meat is ready to be consumed, along with chunks of San Francisco's famous, crunchy, sourdough French bread.

15. *Bobbing* at their berths, the ▶ fishing boats at Fisherman's Wharf await the keen whistle that pipes them off to the fishing grounds outside the Golden Gate. The wharf is a picturesque enclave of boats, restaurants, and specialty stores.

16. *Veteran limejuicer,* built in Glasgow in 1886, the *Balclutha* has been meticulously restored as a museum and draws thousands to prowl its decks. It is one of a fleet of old-time vessels berthed at the foot of Hyde Street.

17. *The figureheads* of long-gone sailing vessels grace the collections of the Maritime Museum, home for ship models, charts, photographs, and maritime gear from the early days of sail and steam.

18. *The grim bulk* of Alcatraz Island looms in mid-bay. The notorious federal prison (1933–63) was used for incorrigibles such as Al Capone and Machine Gun Kelley. Originally a light station, it became a detention camp for Army deserters and prisoners of war before serving as a federal prison. The deactivated facility was invaded in 1969 by Indians who claimed it under a treaty of 1861.

19. *An armada* (*see overleaf*) of sailboats materializes every year at the opening of the sailing season. Three to four hundred skippers sail forth from scores of marinas and yacht harbors and trace a lively minuet over the whitecaps. On such days, the Coast Guard rescues twenty or so inept or unlucky seamen.

20. *The Yacht Harbor* in the Marina district is home port for 700 small craft, ranging from 20-footers to yachts. Of more than 70,000 craft registered in the Greater Bay Area, 10,000 belong to San Franciscans.

21. *Running* before the wind with a ▶ fog bank gathering to leeward, a graceful ketch skims over the choppy surface of the bay.

23. *Tied to the dock* with fragile ▶ heartstrings of confetti, the *S.S. Lurline* makes ready to sail on an excursion, sped bon voyage in a haze of champagne and sentiment.

22. *The S.S. Oriana,* being nudged into dock by powerful tugs, makes eight or nine cruises a year to the South Pacific, Caribbean, and Europe. Passenger vessels such as these, their livelihood threatened by transocean airlines, are enjoying a comeback as floating resort hotels.

24. *Giant aircraft carrier Oriskany,* sailing into the bay after a tour of duty in the South Pacific, is welcomed by the traditional flotilla of spouting fireboats and small craft. The Navy has been an important resident of the port since the 1840's.

25. *Bar pilot,* boarding ship at pilot station outside the Gate, is required by law to guide vessels through the treacherous slot leading into the bay. Bar pilots form a tightly knit fraternity that has been in existence since 1850.

26. *Deadweight* of a 200-ton diesel locomotive being hoisted aboard a Japanese cargo vessel is so substantial that it tips the ship at its berth. Once lofted aboard, the heavy machinery is positioned so the vessel can sail on an even keel.

27. *North Beach,* a yeasty blend of Italy and bohemia, was once actually on the beach before harbor filling moved the shoreline farther into the bay.

THE RICHES OF NORTH BEACH
AND CHINATOWN

Located nextdoor to each other by an accident in history, the Italians in North Beach and the Cantonese in Chinatown share many attributes, even though they came here from worlds apart.

In common, the two enclaves cope with the problems of an ethnic concentration in a small geographic area. Both groups started here as an invasion of young men during the Gold Rush, intent on earning enough to return as wealthy men to their homelands—a dream that few were able to fulfill. Each group brought traditions strongly rooted in the family; each imported intact its own religion, customs, foodstuffs, and cuisine. In time, the charms of each enclave were discovered by outsiders, and today tourists stroll from North Beach to Chinatown and back, dining impartially on cannelloni or chow mein, listening to Verdi arias or Chinese opera, or shopping for silks or Florentine leatherwork.

Little Italy occupies a narrow valley running between Russian and Telegraph hills. Its main street is Columbus Avenue, a diagonal that cuts directly from the old center of town to Fisherman's Wharf. Within this area live eighty thousand Italians, mostly from the northern provinces, many from Sicily. The first to arrive in 1840 were Genoese, who started the fishing industry and then sold out to the Sicilians who came later. The Genoese moved into other endeavors, such as banking, manufacturing, and scavenging. The Sicilians kept up the fishery, and it is they who run the highly successful Fisherman's Wharf and its attendant fleet.

The Italians have brought to the city a warm and fecund way of life, structured around the family and the arts of family living.

28. *Spiritual heart* ot the Italian ▶
colony, Sts. Peter and Paul (built in
1922) provides a graceful setting for
community celebrations.

SAN FRANCISCO ⚜

Their shops and restaurants offer tantalizing fare for the gourmet, the venturesome diner, or the person who simply desires an authentic plate of spaghetti.

The story of Chinatown, next door to Little Italy, has not always been a happy one, although it would be difficult to guess this from a casual observation of the present scene. The area was settled by young men from Canton who migrated to the gold fields to make a quick fortune and then return home. Most of them never made it. Hundreds remained in San Francisco, sequestered into a few square blocks where they were forced to eke out a living at menial chores.

On top of an already compressed population, thousands more poured in during the 1860's, imported by labor contractors to build the Central Pacific Railroad. A wholly male society, hopelessly estranged from their homeland, with no economic prospects, and separated from the Americans by a cultural abyss and by language barriers, they were steeped in poverty and many took to crime. For several decades, Chinatown was a witches' brew of evildoing that was finally wiped out by the fire of 1906, which forced rebuilding, resettling, and needed reforms.

Gradually the Chinese solved their problems, gained acceptance from the dominant community, and developed Grant Avenue into a little piece of Canton, which attracted first the curious, then the appreciative tourist. Today the Chinese community is respected as a rich cultural and commercial asset to the city. Its colorfu lshops offer an unparalleled selection of oriental goods, and its dozens of restaurants a delectable sample of Cantonese cookery.

30. *Blessing of the Fleet* on the first Sunday in October is an ancient ceremony brought from Italy by the Sicilian fishermen. The ritual starts at Sts. Peter and Paul and is followed by a parade to Fisherman's Wharf.

29. *Christopher Columbus,* sword stuck in the pier, doles out brightly colored beads to the Indians in the annual Columbus Day (October 12) pageant, an engaging Italian celebration.

32. *Redolent of garlic,* the delicatessens of North Beach display a rich variety of good eating: bologna and cheeses, finocchio, salami, panettoni, canoli, and in spring the supreme delicacy, capretto (suckling kid) are featured in every window.

◀31. *The reel-in clothesline,* a fixture of the private side of most row houses, displays a cross section of life in North Beach: scarlet parochial school sweaters, scores of snowy diapers, and a line of grade school togs.

47

33. *A row* of psychedelic-colored store fronts and wry business names identify Upper Grant, a bohemian offshoot of North Beach.

37. *Broadway (see overleaf),* ablaze with clamorous neon, concentrates dozens of bars, night clubs, strip joints, and first-rate restaurants in four long blocks along the southern edge of North Beach. It offers a mix of entertainment from tawdry to topflight. Famous for originating the topless phenomenon.

34—36. *Tomorrow's* arts and crafts— posters, paintings, books, and food stuffs, leatherwork, ceramics, and jewelry are displayed and sold in this outpost of Hippieland.

38. *In Chinatown,* even the phone booths have pagoda roofs. This one is beside old St. Mary's Church, an 1854 landmark of Grant Avenue.

39. *Waiting in the rain,* the St. Mary's Chinese Girls' Drum Corps listens for the whistle which will send them forth on a march through Chinatown; the corps has been in demand for 27 years to grace Chinese festivals and civic parades.

40. *Sun Yat Sen* in stainless steel and rose-colored granite, a tribute to the founder of the Chinese Republic by sculptor Beniamino Bufano, gazes benignly down on tranquil St. Mary's Park—once the setting for an iniquitous concentration of vice.

53

41. *Smoked chicken* and pork, dan-
gling in a store window, are basic to
many Chinese recipes; in the steam
trays below: sweet-sour pork, bean
sprouts, mushrooms, and water chest-
nuts.

44. *Spectacular feature (see overleaf)* of ▶ the week-long festival of Chinese New Year is the 50-man dragon that rampages through the streets.

42. *Windows* decorated for New Year feature poems, azaleas, and hangings of red—the traditional New Year color.

43. *Outdoor display* at a market offers ingredients for a feast: bamboo shoots, ginger root, Chinese cabbage, mustard greens, and cucumbers.

45.   *The Chinatown* that most tourists remember is the eight-block section of Grant Avenue that is lined with shops and restaurants. A wide variety of oriental goods is sold here, ranging from cheap souvenirs to exquisite works of art. Fine eating places along the avenue and in side streets serve predominantly Cantonese food.

46.   *Entrance gate* to Chinatown marks the southern boundary at Bush Street. Decorative materials for the structure, including green roof tiles and the dragons, were shipped from Taiwan as a gift of the Republic of China.

47. *The evolving skyline* of the downtown area is changing daily as newer and taller buildings convert the business district into a western Manhattan. When this photograph was taken in 1969, the Bank of America building towered above its neighbors— but even taller structures are taking shape.

DOWNTOWN—WHERE OLD IS NEW

The thump of the pile driver, as insistent as a pounding headache, echoes through the downtown area and is likely to do so for many years to come. The sound is long overdue, for sections of the area have been decaying for decades, and replacement has been inevitable if the city's core were ever to regain its lost vitality.

The bold new plans are just beginning to reveal themselves in steel and concrete. A walk through the Golden Gateway (see page 88), first of the "new look" in urban architecture, shows the scene of the future. Here, the new buildings are located far apart, with ample air and ground space between, and connected by elevated malls, plazas, and bridges. The mundane business of traffic, deliveries, merchandising, and parking take place at ground level, while the pedestrians circulate at the second story, free of contact with motor vehicles. The elevated malls of the Gateway will in time extend over much of the old business district, and visitors will be able to walk from north of Broadway to south of Market without once stepping on mother earth or dodging an automobile. Traffic will flow through canyons below, spanned by graceful bridges.

Such a massive revitalization of downtown is explained by a fact peculiar to San Francisco: the city is already filled to the brim with buildings and there is no place to go but up. Unlike the newer cities in the proliferating suburbs, there is no room and property values are too exorbitant to permit building vast shopping centers in the outskirts that may drain business away from the central area; thus, the commercial core is likely to remain where it has always been, in the northeast corner of the city.

48. *California Street* is fast becoming ▶
a second "Wall Street of the West,"
rivaling Montgomery Street in the
number of banks, insurance companies, and investment firms.

SAN FRANCISCO ⚜

Such enormous undertakings will take decades to complete, and
in the long meanwhile there are dozens of places to explore on foot
or by cable car downtown and in nearby neighborhoods, where one
can savor the unique flavor of the city's business community and
dine or shop in interesting or amusing surroundings.

An off-again-on-again ride on a California Street cable car takes
the visitor through the heart of the financial district, the power
center of the West, past the Montgomery Street canyon, long known
as the "Wall Street of the West" for its saturation with financial
institutions. Along the way are samples of the new urban landscaping that is bringing plants, bushes, fountains, and dry landscaping
to the ground level of many business buildings. At Union Square,
heart of the shopping district since the Civil War, are dozens of fine
stores and the stately St. Francis Hotel, a hostelry that is traditional
for its luxury cuisine and accommodation.

On the fringes of downtown, some of the most interesting shopping and professional areas are located in old, pre-fire buildings
that have been lovingly resurrected or deftly modernized with the
latest interior design. A stroll through Jackson Square on the site
of the Gold Rush city, along Union Street where a Victorian
neighborhood has been converted to shops, and, near the northern
waterfront, through the terraces of the Cannery and Ghirardelli
Square, reveal a beguiling assortment of boutiques, bars, restaurants, yarn shops, import outlets, decorator shops, and professional
offices that offer a rewarding treat for the visitor who is interested
in seeing how the past can be made to smartly serve the present.

◀49. *Downtown,* old style: heroic
Mechanics Monument, by deaf-mute
sculptor Douglas Tilden, has marked
the corner of Montgomery and Market
Streets since 1894.

50. *Downtown,* new style: windows
on the shaded side of the Bank of
America building act as mirrors,
reflecting the New England style home
of Fireman's Fund Insurance.

51. *A paved oasis* in the heart of downtown, Zellerbach Plaza introduces a park of pebbles, stone, plant materials, and running water in an open acre at the base of the skyscraper and is popular with noontime brown-baggers.

52. *Dining* in a setting of traditional ▶ elegance is offered by the famous Garden Court of the Sheraton Palace Hotel, a replica of an inner court where guests once alighted from their carriages in the illustrious predecessor of the present hotel built in 1878.

53. *Sidewalk flower stands,* charming nosegays in the downtown area, have displayed their bright fragrance for two generations.

54. *Forceful design* of a gallery by Frank Lloyd Wright highlights Maiden Lane.

55. *Ablaze* for the Christmas season, ▶ Union Square is thronged during the holidays with shoppers, loafers, and pigeons to the ninth power.

56. *Typical* of the antique buildings deftly resurrected to a new life in Jackson Square is this old theater, built in 1868 and now an attorney's office.

57. *Habitat* of interior decorators and wholesale furniture dealers, Jackson Square (not a square but an area once the bawdy Barbary Coast) is packed with display rooms open mainly to the trade. Buildings date from the 1860's.

58. *A bright swirl* of color down Gold Street in old San Francisco invites patrons to an art gallery, a bar, a pungent vinegar works.

61. *The Cannery* offers its ► own blend of contemporary nostalgia. Metamorphosed from a Del Monte fruit cannery (1906—ca. 1941), the monolithic brick structure reopened in 1967 with terraces, flying balustrades, bridges, and balconies—a massive piece of walk-through sculpture. A glass elevator enables visitors to enjoy a bay vista as they ascend to the shops in the upper reaches.

59. *Where past is present:* an imaginative transformation of an 1878 chocolate factory into an ingratiating shopping and dining complex, Ghirardelli Square steps down the hill to the waterfront in a brick cascade of shops, restaurants, and terraces.

60. *Festooned* with lights, the old factory takes on a carnival air in the misty dark.

◄62. *Gingerbread* buildings of the Victorian era provide the setting for another successful resurrection of the past on outer Union Street, formerly home to the dairy herds of the young city.

63. *Small shops* specializing in art objects, brassware, paintings, fine clothing, wines, cheeses, flowers, and food line Union Street.

64. *Every* available bit of space has been utilized for merchandising. Alleys lead to antique shops and florists, set up in former carriage houses; upstairs are bookshops and first-rate galleries.

65. *A blend* of tomorrow and yesterday, the shops, restaurants, and accommodations at the Japanese Trade and Cultural Center offer goods and services with a long tradition and some that are keyed to the most advanced technology.

66. *Westerners* enjoy the novelty of "dining off the floor" and savoring the authentic cuisine served in the city's Japanese restaurants.

67. *The stylized Peace Pagoda,* recognizable symbol of the Trade and Cultural Center, is dedicated to international goodwill.

SAN FRANCISCO IN RESIDENCE

To sample the unique character of residential San Francisco, a visitor need only to explore Telegraph and Russian hills and drive out Pacific Avenue towards the ocean to gain meaningful impressions about living space in this unusual city.

First, there is the fact of hill living itself, a facet of life that offers compensations and inconveniences in nearly equal measure. Hill living is a daily physical challenge. Each ascent, even if it is only to carry laundry from the car or post a letter, is a little achievement. Each descent is an exercise in exquisite muscular control, especially in the rain and doubly so in high heels (usually carried in a handbag for steep descents). All of this without help from the faithful family car which is parked awry on a sloping street, often some distance from the house.

Yet, for all the inconvenience, San Franciscans willingly pay a premium for living on a hill, the steeper the better, because of the rewarding view it usually offers. The premium may vary from a few dollars extra rent for a handkerchief-sized view of the bay to several hundred dollars for a commanding panorama from a high-rise apartment or an aerie on Telegraph Hill.

Another truth that the observant traveler may discern is the small size of the average row house, many of them built on twenty-five-foot lots. The narrow lot got its start in Spanish days when plots were assigned to the first settlers. The standard allotment was ten *varas* in width—approximately twenty-five feet—and this was picked up by later developers who applied it throughout a great deal of the city. There are still some tiny houses, one lot wide, tucked in between double-lot homes that are regarded as rare finds by those lucky enough to track them down.

Not only are the homes small, but hundreds display the exuberant decoration and window framing that identifies Victorian era construction. Local residents prize these old structures, some of which were built by fond fathers as wedding gifts for daughters, for their spaciousness, solid construction, and conscientious workmanship. Modernization, on the inside, of the kitchen and bath, wiring, plumbing, and heating is contrasted, on the outside, by meticulous preservation of every last curlicue, often enhanced with decorator colors.

These older homes are also noteworthy for the city's residential trademark—the bay window. Other cities have them too, but probably nowhere else have they flowered as in this city. Bay windows were the main decorative element open to builders of row houses, but, even more important, this type of window was the life source for sun and warmth in a cool and foggy climate, and symbolically acquired importance in its own right as a means to comfortable living.

Of course, not every San Franciscan lives in a Victorian house perched on a hill. A surprising seventy percent of the residents live in rented quarters, mostly flats and apartments. High-rise apartments, man-made hills if you will, stand on top of hills or in lieu of hills, offering a bay view as their main inducement. The emergence of first-class apartments downtown in the Golden Gateway, surrounded by looming skyscrapers only two blocks from the bay, foreshadows a trend towards downtown living. On the outskirts, developers are still erecting row houses, built fire wall to fire wall in long strings that, at a distance, resemble white freight trains.

69—71. *Hills* are a daily challenge in the lives of most San Franciscans, who are inured to parking at such amazing angles, ascending endless steps, and avoiding streets too steep to drive up.

72. *Since 1873,* the cable cars have lurched turtlelike up hill and down dale at an implacable 9 miles per hour. Originally installed to provide easy access to the luxury homes on top of Nob Hill, cable lines eventually covered 297 miles until destroyed by fire in 1906 or replaced by electric streetcars.

73. *The Hyde Street* cable car, descending to Victorian Park, was first put on the line in the early 1890's. A San Francisco institution, the cable car is now designated a National Historical Monument—the only one on wheels. ▶

74. *Unique feature* of the system is a ▶ complex system of pulleys and guides that permits the endless cable to follow the contours of the hills. Access to the mechanism is through numerous steel doors in the pavement.

75. *The staunch* little cars, designed ▶ to hold 30 passengers, often start out loaded to capacity and pick up dozens more who cling with simian tenacity.

78. *Grace Cathe-*▶
dral, seeming to vanish under the beetling cliff of a high-rise apartment house, is the seat of the Protestant Episcopal Church in San Francisco. Construction of the beautiful edifice was started in 1914 and is still incomplete. On the right, brownstone quarters of the Pacific Union Club behind an ornate, solid bronze fence are the only Nob Hill mansion to have escaped destruction in the 1906 fire.

76. *Two elegant hostelries* adorn the crest of Nob Hill: the Mark Hopkins (1925), above, and the Fairmont (1907) across the street compete vigorously for carriage trade.

77. *Children* scamper around the Fountain of the Turtles in Huntington Park. The copy of a 16th century Roman piece was given to the city by the family of Charles Crocker, a railroad tycoon.

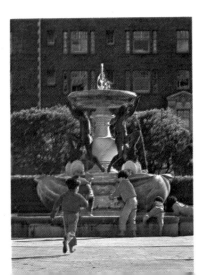

79. *Lombard Street* corkscrew is a favorite San Francisco treat for newcomers. In one steep block, the brick-paved street drops down the east face of Russian Hill in eight switchbacks.

80—81. *Telegraph Hill,* named for a marine semaphor that once crowned its crest, was originally a shanty town and goat pasture, but is now a prime, if vertiginous, place to live. Its flanks are encrusted with apartments, homes, and tiny dwellings. Accessible on the east only by steps, its summit is easily reached by car from the west. On top, Coit Tower provides a sweeping view of the bay.

82. *Foretaste* of things to come, the Golden Gateway Development was first of the downtown complexes to combine living, business, and shopping in one. The widely separated buildings are connected by an elevated pedestrian mall embellished with plantings, fountains, and sculptures.

83. *A cascade of* diamonds falls in the Fountain of the Four Seasons, an enchanting adornment of a privately owned park in the downtown's Golden Gateway.

84. *A dandelion* of jets, this luminous fountain is in Alcoa Plaza at the Gateway.

85—93. *Bay windows* in variety are an architectural trademark of the city. Designed originally to extract every ray of sunshine and molecule of warmth from the foggy air, they appeared by the thousands during the building booms of the 1890's.

94. *Shingled row houses* facing the forbidden grounds of the Presidio visually trespass on the forested military preserve.

95. *In a city* with little growing space (*see overleaf*), homes are packed wall to wall. Outdoor living space, if any, is confined to back gardens with only token plantings on the streetside, as can be seen in this view from above Mount Davidson and Twin Peaks.

96. *Visitors romp* with an obliging piece of kinetic sculpture, *The Rotozaza*, at the San Francisco Museum of Art, a lively contemporary institution.

OFFERINGS IN THE ARTS

Visitors with an interest in the arts have been able to find excitement in San Francisco ever since Gold Rush days, for this is a city that has always been friendly to artists, musicians, and writers, and has helped boost more than one to national prominence.

In this cordial atmosphere, several musical organizations produce noteworthy concert series each year. Unique among municipalities, the city sponsors its own symphony (founded in 1911) and helps support a ballet company (1933) and an opera company (1923), all of which perform in a city-owned opera house built in 1932. Ranked by some critics as among the nation's foremost, these companies stage high quality productions, mostly within the classic tradition.

Likewise a patron of the fine arts, the city has its own arts commission that sponsors an annual art show, complete with awards and scholarships, and serves as an aesthetic watchdog to screen the designs for all civic buildings, fountains, monuments, murals, and statuary. Three major museums—one run by the city—combine to offer an unparalleled spectrum of art, from conventional to unorthodox. A number of small galleries supplement the large ones with highly selective exhibits.

Long known as a good theater town, San Francisco supports three active legitimate stages in the Geary, Curran, and Marine's Memorial theaters, a scattering of little theaters, and a half dozen intimate stages noted for their good-humored but barbed criticism of established ways. A string of raffish theaters on Broadway and its side streets carry on a pallid continuation of the wicked theater of the old Barbary Coast, a phenomenon of iniquitous entertainment.

97. *Serene,* monumental, symmetrical, the California Palace of the Legion of Honor houses a mixture of 17th and 18th century art, plus galleries devoted to exciting traveling exhibits. In the entry court, Auguste Rodin's

The Thinker ponders, one of five original casts. Modeled after the Palais de la Légion d'Honneur in Paris, the building was given to the city by a wealthy sugar-growing family in memory of California's World War I dead.

98. *Guide* interprets a figure of the Hindu deity, Vishnu, to attentive art lovers in the M. H. de Young Memorial Museum, noted for its extraordinary collection of oriental art loaned by Avery Brundage, art collector and Olympics czar.

99. *Oldest* (1894) and most popular art museum (1,500,000 visitors yearly), the de Young houses a collection ranging from old masters to works by Californians. In Golden Gate Park, the museum faces the Music Concourse and the Academy of Sciences.

99

100. *Annual outpouring* of self-expression surrounds and invades the reflecting pool at the Civic Center. Sponsored by the city's art commission, the show attracts hundreds of artists and yields a prodigious display of paintings and tapestries, sculptures and ceramics, and inventions. In 1969 there were 2,100 items on display, spanning the spectrum from excellent to awful. In the background looms the majestic presence of the city hall, a distinguished example of classic architecture completed in 1915 to replace a predecessor "held together with more graft than mortar" that had disintegrated in 48 seconds in the 1906 earthquake.

101—102. *Pride* of the city is the American Conservatory Theater, a talented and venturesome group that has brought some of the most compelling current dramas to the city. *A Flea in Her Ear*, shown here, opened in San Francisco and was later taken to New York for a reversal of the customary migration of stage successes from Broadway to the West Coast.

104. *A Christmas tradition* since 1943, ▶ Tchaikovsky's *Nutcracker* is produced by the San Francisco Ballet as a holiday treat for children. Given in its entirety, the ballet is a beguiling confection, complete with dancing mice, toy soldiers, real cannon, and a raspberry juice fountain.

103. *Dance* of the swans is deftly choreographed and enhanced by romantic lighting.

105. *Imaginative sets,* such as this one for Mozart's *Magic Flute,* have characterized the productions of the San Francisco Opera Company since its inception in 1923.

106. *Home* of the opera and symphony, the imposing War Memorial Opera House (1932) was created by the same architect who designed the majestic city hall. The building was the setting for the launching of the United Nations in April 1945.

107.   *Mile-long* Ocean Beach attracts throngs to its sands on sunny weekends and an intrepid few to its chilly and treacherous surf.

HIGHLIGHTS ON THE 49-MILE DRIVE

Not all of San Francisco's sights are crowded into the northeast corner of the city. Outside this compact area, there are a number of places well worth experiencing—some that appeal to the nature lover, some to the sportsman, many to families seeking the tonic of a day in the open air.

Most of these points are located around the perimeter of the city, all on the 49-mile Drive, a carefully plotted route that visitors can follow in their automobiles with the help of a map (see page 9) and an eagle-eyed member of the family as navigator.

In the southeastern corner of the city, Candlestick Park attracts die-hard fans of the San Francisco Giants and Forty-niners to its windy bleachers. In the southwestern corner, a concentration of outdoor attractions draws a variety of outdoorsmen to a golf course, a boating and fishing lake, and the world's largest outdoor swimming pool. Next to it is a modest zoo, stocked with animals in open-air enclosures.

Along the ocean front, a sandy beach stretches for three miles, pounded by a chilly surf with a strong undertow beyond the breakers; and across a wide esplanade, Playland lures children of all ages to a gaudy array of Coney Island concessions. Up the hill, the route passes the Cliff House (1908), a lineal descendent of two predecessors that burned to the ground. Here tourists can stop to gaze through coin-operated, mist-dimmed binoculars at raucous sea lions disporting on Seal Rocks four hundred feet offshore.

The forested grounds of the one thousand seven hundred-acre Presidio offer a bosky maze in which it is easy to get lost if the

109

navigator becomes inattentive. A fortified post since 1776 when the Spaniards planted guns on the cliff, there is little here to see except the heavily restored adobe Officers' Club (1776) and Fort Point (1861), down at the water's edge almost hidden under an anchorage of the Golden Gate Bridge. Open occasionally to visitors, this vast, many-chambered fortress protected the harbor from foreign men-of-war for eighty years but was never called upon to prove its defenses. The fort's rusted bars, chains, and iron doors give a hint of what could happen to the lofty bridge overhead if the painters ever abandoned it to the elements.

Just outside the Presidio gates stands the Palace of Fine Arts, mirrored in a reed-grown reflecting pool. A remarkable period piece dating from the exposition of 1915, it was recently rebuilt in permanent materials to be used as a cultural center.

By far the most compelling stop along the 49-Mile Drive is Golden Gate Park, the world's largest man-made park. Within its five square miles of landscaped grounds are enough walks, drives, bridle paths, arboreta, ponds, and scientific and artistic institutions to engage every taste. Sports enthusiasts can watch or participate in polo, flycasting, track, football, archery. Families can bring their picnic baskets, spread out on the spacious lawns and introduce their children to live buffalo, ducks, geese, and countless seagulls, or take them to see the heavens re-created in a planetarium, watch myriads of fish in an aquarium, or gaze in awe at a stuffed Kodiak bear three times larger than Smokey.

The great park is a monument to a remarkable Scotsman, John McLaren, who took charge of a preserve of rolling sand dunes in 1887, and, conquering natural and political obstacles, created the park as we know it today.

108. *Candlestick Park,* home of the San Francisco Giants (nee New York Giants), is legendary for its fogs, chill, and mischievous winds that can straighten a curve pitch, loft a two-bagger over the fence, or drive a fly ball straight up. The stadium is also home for the Fortyniners football team.

109. *A carbon copy* of Fort Sumter, old Fort Point is a fascinating shell to explore on the days when it is open to visitors. Built in 1861 on the site of the original Spanish battery, its galleries were armed with big, bulbous cannon that were never fired in anger and were all eventually melted down.

110. *The Palace of Fine Arts* is a fine sentimental trophy of the Panama-Pacific Exposition of 1915. Originally a temporary structure of plaster and chicken wire, it somehow held together for half a century and was permanently restored in 1968 at a cost of $6 million.

111. *Weather permitting,* the Municipal Band gives free concerts on Sundays and holidays in the Music Concourse in Golden Gate Park.

112—113. *Recreation* for all temperaments can be pursued in Golden Gate Park. In one area, rugby players may be bulldozing their way through a scrum; in another, remote-controlled model ships will be sailing among unconcerned gulls and ducks on a quiet lake.

115

115. *Sculptured porpoises* cavort in▶ front of Steinhart Aquarium, which features dolphins, talking fish, and 12,000 smaller fry in huge glass tanks.

114. *Oldest* scientific institution on the West Coast (1853), the California Academy of Sciences offers public exhibits in four major divisions: wildlife of North America and of Africa, a planetarium, and an aquarium.

116. *Pol-larded* syc-amores and elms make a gold canopy over the Music Con-course in the autumn.

117

117.   *The tranquil pools,* winding paths, shrines, and bridges of the Japanese Tea Garden in the park have enchanted several generations of visitors since it was opened in 1894 as part of the Japanese Village at the California Midwinter International Exposition.

118.   *In contrast* to the immaculate landscaping of the tea garden, great green pastures invite the stroller, lounger, or picnicker, and scampering dogs and children. There are no "Keep off the Grass" signs in Golden Gate Park.

119—120. (*See above and opposite*). *Modeled* after the Royal Conservatories at Kew Gardens, England, the Conservatory dates from 1883. The mammoth greenhouse shelters a varied collection of jungle plants from all the world's tropical areas.

121. *A somber memorial* to President Garfield dating from 1885 serves today as a popular rest stop for the young.

120

122. *Packed* into the southwest corner of the city are bridle paths, a golf course, two boating lakes, a zoo, an enormous swimming pool (populated only on the warmest days). Over it all can be heard the muted thunder of the surf as it rolls against the continent's leading edge.